D1486938

TICKLE THE TOES
TOUCH THE HEART
CHANGE THE MIND

Lessons for growing your business through storytelling

by Chuck Mefford

Printed in the United States of America

First Printing, 2019

ISBN 9781513637457

BrandsFormation©
Argyle, Texas
brandsformation.com

Dedication

God, thank you for your undeserved grace and unconditional love, and for these five angels you have watching over me.

Charles D. and Gayle Mefford. Thank you for pointing me in the right direction and loving me through every wrong turn I made. I wish I could see you one more time to thank you and hug you.

Bob and Doris Hale. Thank you for your support and love. You are incredible people, and I love you like my own Mom and Dad.

To my wife, Roann, thank you for rocking my world. I am living a dream and loving it.

Table of Contents

Introduction

STOP SHOUTING SALES. START SHARING. You're frustrated. You run a good business. Your products and/or services are humming along great, but sales are still flat. You've dumped your hard-earned money into traditional and digital advertising, and yet, you still feel like "the best kept secret in town."

You're overwhelmed with endless marketing choices and more competition, and you have no idea how to break through the clutter. After working with American business owners for over 40 years, I feel your pain, and I've seen this story play over and over again.

Breathe in slowly. Stop. Hold. Now exhale. The good news is you're in the right place. I will show you how you can grow your business through storytelling just as I have done with thousands of small businesses across America.

The first question you need to ask is, "What does my product/service do for my customer?" If you took more than three seconds to think about it, and then gave a vague, confusing, or longer-than-one-sentence answer, I have good news and bad news. The good news ... your business doesn't suck. The bad news ... your storytelling does.

How does ...

a kitchen cabinet maker go from $200,000 to $4+ million in annual sales?

a dentist blow away the competition and grow from $750,000 to over $10 million a year?

a pest control business that started with a truck and a spray can grow to $5+ million in sales?

Storytelling, that's how! Okay ... they were (and still are) great business people with good products and services to start. However, understanding who they are to the customer and telling that story over and over again is how they became household names and began blowing the doors off their sales projections to make huge market share increases!

So, stop shouting sales and start telling stories. People love good stories. Storytelling, as a marketing strategy, is the best way to break through the clutter in a memorable way. Stories enter the heart and change the mind in a way that "advertising" never, ever will.

You have a good story to tell; every business does. To help you uncover your story, I've identified eight simple, yet powerful lessons for building your story and boosting your bottom line.

It's time to tickle the toes, touch the heart, and change the mind.

All hat, no cattle

THE CEO OF A NATIONAL DOG FOOD BRAND ARRIVED AT A COMPANY-WIDE, EMERGENCY MEETING HE HAD CALLED. You could hear a pin drop as he walked to the podium at McCormick Place Convention Hall filled with suppliers; vendors; salespeople; marketing folks; and distribution, production, and shipping people. He wasted no time. "The best scientists developed this dog food. We're on TV and radio all year long, and we have a brilliant digital strategy. Our sales force is the best in the biz. We have the approval of the American Dog Food Society. Heck, we even advertised on the Super Bowl this year! Would someone please explain to me 'Why sales are tanking!'"

Long silence, and then, from the back of the room, a lone voice cried out, "The dogs don't like it!"

In Texas, we call this "All hat, no cattle!" A polite, Southern way of saying, "He's full of it!" The walk doesn't match the talk.

Lesson #1

Your brand is your promise to your customer. Don't make promises you can't deliver. Your business has to be good before you begin telling your story. Everything, from your product or service, your physical location, your bathrooms, your staff, your customer service, your return policy – each of these consumer touchpoints (and others) – needs to live up to the story you are telling consumers. Nothing will take a mediocre business down quicker than inviting people in for an experience that doesn't live up to your promise.

Lesson 2

What we can learn from a bank robber

IT'S CRAZY, MEDICAL STUDENTS LEARNING FROM A BANK ROBBER! Whaaat? It's true, med students are often taught Sutton's Law as a metaphor for focusing on a "most likely diagnosis," rather than wasting time and resources searching all possibilities. "Sutton" was Willie Sutton, a successful bank robber in his day, stealing more than $2 million over his 44-year career. He was convicted of robbing a bank in 1950 and sentenced to 30 -120 years. On his way to Attica State Prison,

a reporter shouted at Willie, "Why do you rob banks?" Willie reportedly replied, "That's where the money is."
After all these years, it's still a great illustration for the power of focus and getting the best results, quicker. So, what does Sutton's Law have to do with your marketing? I'm glad you asked.

The big guys like Nike, Yeti, and Apple got to be leaders in their categories by focusing their money and their efforts toward the biggest group of potential customers.

Let's talk about the two buyer groups:

Transactional buyers make quick decisions based on low price. They respond to discounts and deals. These folks think short-term.

Relational buyers make decisions based on value, trust and loyalty. They like to feel connected. This group thinks long-term.

If you are in the food, entertainment, or another business category with a quick-turn product cycle, the transactional buyer is your sweet spot. This group of buyers is motivated by sales, deals and discounts. So, they will stick with you only until they find a better price somewhere else. *Low price* as a long-term strategy is what I like to call the ***springboard into bankruptcy plan***!

On the other hand, if your product cycles over years, your money and efforts should focus on the Relational buyer. Relational buyers are not motivated by sales. Relational buyers are all about value and connection and long-term relationships.

My mentor and good friend, Don Jacobs, created a "Customer Marketing Pyramid" that dramatizes this point.

Transactional

NOW BUYER
next 30 days

READY BUYER
next 12 months

Relational

FUTURE BUYER
next 2-7 years

Fundamental business principal: For most businesses, 90% of their customers will come from the bottom group on the pyramid, the Future/Relational buyers.

Fundamental business mistake: Throwing your hard- earned money at the top 10% of the pyramid and missing the boat with 90% of your future customers by not focusing your money and talking to them.

Who are you talking to? Are you "going where the money is"? Take a look at your product cycle, and answer these two questions:

- Which group represents the most sales for your business?
- Where are you focusing your marketing dollars and efforts?

Lesson #2

Stop "throwing money at everyone and hoping something sticks!" Instead, *go where the money is*! Focus your marketing on the group that represents the most potential customers for your business. Big brands, be they national, regional or local build their brands by having ongoing conversations with Future/Relational buyers. Trust is important to this group and you build trust with them over time through storytelling. *Go where the money is* and start making connections now. The next time these consumers need the product or service you offer, they will think of you first because you have already made a connection with them. You've tickled the toes, touched the heart and changed the mind!

Lesson 3

Be like Mike and Melvin

YOU ONLY HAVE TO SAY *BE LIKE MIKE*, **AND DARN NEAR EVERYONE ON THE PLANET KNOWS YOU'RE TALKING ABOUT #23 MICHAEL "MJ" JORDAN.** He was a leader in a league filled with world-class athletes. He practiced and played at the highest level, and off the court, he did (and does) amazing things for charitable work. MJ captured our hearts and became a hero to an entire generation. Gatorade knew that if the world's best basketball player drank Gatorade, we would as well, because we would want to *Be Like Mike*.

Melvin, on the other hand, never won a national basketball championship, but he was the MJ of his field (and my Bumpa)! Melvin was a leading farmer and seed salesman. He was up every day before the first rooster crowed, making sure his corn rows were straight as an arrow because that was a measure of being the best. Melvin invested in the latest equipment; his farm and his barns were meticulously cared for and organized. Melvin left nothing to chance in order to yield the best corn in DeKalb County.

Later on, Melvin's reputation as a leading farmer gave him instant credibility that helped make him Top DeKalb Seed Salesman, year after year. He sold tons of XL45 seed corn, all because those other farmers wanted to *Be Like Melvin*.

Melvin did have one more thing in common with MJ. He was also a basketball player. In the first-ever Harlem Globetrotters game on January 27, 1927 in Hinckley, IL, on the opposing side, a fierce opponent, Melvin Morsch. My Bumpa. My Hero.

"Leadership is like a string. Pull the string, and it will follow wherever you wish. Push it, and it will go nowhere."
– Dwight D. Eisenhower

Lesson #3

Leaders lead by example. You earn leadership by getting good at something and developing a reputation for it over time. As a marketing strategy, Leadership works because it appeals to our sense of "wanting what others have." And when other people say we should try something, there's nothing more powerful. It's why "high ratings and likes" (word of mouth) are so important. Are you a Leader? If so, congrats! Your hard work has paid off! Now, go tell consumers that you are the best, you are #1. You can do it without being obnoxious. Plant your flag! Let Leadership be your strategy to build your brand, generate customers, sell more, and increase your profits.

Facts tell, stories sell

PRINCE OF TROY STEALS AWAY A GREEK KING'S WIFE, HELENA! War ensues! After a fruitless 10-year siege to enter the city of Troy, the Greeks come up with the outstanding idea of building a huge, wooden horse as a peace offering for the people of Troy. It ends badly when a bunch of angry, hairy, Greek dudes pile out of the belly of the wooden horse and take back Helena, trashing Troy on the way out.

We all know the story of the Trojan Horse, but do you know in what century it took place or how long it lasted?

You've probably heard the story of the biggest, baddest, most expensive ocean liner ever built colliding with a giant iceberg. The ship that promised to be unsinkable sank to the bottom of the North Atlantic, killing more than half of its passengers.

You may know the story of the Titanic, but do you know what year it happened? The number of passengers aboard? The number of victims or survivors?

The stories of the Trojan Horse and Titanic have been told and retold, over many years, in countless articles, TV shows, documentaries, and movies. We remember the stories, but rarely can we recall the facts and figures surrounding the stories.

In Springfield, MO, if you ask, "Who builds kitchens in the tradition of their slightly obsessive Amish ancestors?," you're going to hear an almost universal answer: Kitchenland USA. Brad Schrock and his crew are responsible for thousands of dream kitchens in and around Springfield.

In the beginning, Brad did what every other cabinet guy was doing: advertised "big sale of the month," pushing a certain promotion each month. There are two things immediately wrong with this scenario: 1) trying to "predict the moment of need" is impossible, and 2) because every other cabinet company was also shouting "sale of the month!," no business stood out. This kind of "sameness" causes us to tune out.

Instead of beating the "sales drum," Brad and his wife Amanda began an ongoing conversation about what his cabinets do to make the lives of Moms (and Dads!) easier and better. How his cabinets were built for the long haul with Amish craftsmanship.

Now, when a homeowner is ready for new cabinets in Springfield, she thinks of Kitchenland USA. Why? Because Kitchenland tickled her toes, touched her heart, and now owns a spot in her mind.

Lesson #4

Our brains tune out and forget facts and "sales."
Our brains tune into and remember good stories.
Don't tell me you "sell mattresses"; tell me how your
mattresses will help me sleep like a baby and make my
life better! That's when the connection begins. Once you
make a connection, you no longer have to predict the
moment of need and create "SALES!" around it. Instead,
you create a connection and trust long before
consumers need your product or service.

23

5

Pull the car over

REMEMBER TRAVELING DOWN THE ROAD WITH YOUR FAMILY ON VACATION AND PASSING A HERD OF COWS IN A PASTURE? Did you ever come to a screeching halt, and say, "Hey kids, wow, look at those cows!" Most likely not. Why? Probably because cows are a dime a dozen; you've seen one ... However, imagine that you happen to drive past a purple cow. There would be surprise, shock, and even squeals of delight coming from your car. That's worth "pulling the car over"!

– Inspired by marketing guru Seth Godin's book, *Purple Cow: Transform Your Business by Being Remarkable* (and his other must-read books)

Godin's story for how our brains are conditioned to overlook the ordinary, but "pull over" for the extraordinary is the very reason YOU HAVE TO BE DIFFERENT. He asks "What makes you remarkable?" In my System, I ask "What is your Difference Maker?" What makes you better? What truly sets your business or service apart from every other competitor? What can you claim that none of your competitors can? That's your Difference Maker (DM)! That's what will make your business worth "pulling over for!" A clearly defined DM is critical because you will dramatize it, over and over again, in your storytelling. Think of your DM as *what you want to be known for*.

If you are developing your DM, these questions will help get you on your way.

- What do you do better than your competition?
- What are you currently doing to WOW your customers?
- Why would customers want to shop you over your competitors?
- Why are your long-term customers still with you?
- What do you offer that the competition can't or doesn't?

Does something jump out? Are you beginning to see a common thread? Don't underestimate anything; something simple may be just the thing that makes your business stand out from the competition. For your DM to be a "true Difference Maker," it needs to be something that your competitors can't also claim.

Lesson #5

The old American Express campaign was "Don't Leave Home Without It." In business, when it comes to your **Difference Maker**, "Don't Market Your Business Without It." Let me be clear, if you don't know what makes your business different or better, consumers won't either. Without a clearly defined DM in your marketing, you might as well be just another cow in a field that goes unnoticed by passersby. But, once you have your DM identified, you can build your story around it – set yourself apart from competitors and give consumers a reason to "pull the car over" for your business.

Follow the Three Fs: Fit, Feel, Faithful

LOU HAD JUST LOST HIS JOB. His wife was pregnant with their third child. They had just spent their last dollar on a new house in a new town. It was, to say the least, the lowest point in his life. Then, his wife gave him a book on goal setting. Lou began to read, and the more he read, the more excited he got! He went back to his wife, list in hand, and said, "Look, Honey, I've read the entire book, and I've set 108 goals for my life ... jump out of a plane, ride in a submarine, meet the President of the United States, be head coach of Notre Dame and win the National Championship. I'm going to do every one of these suckers!"

When Lou Holtz heard his wife's response, "How about get a job?," he replied, "Very well then, 109, get a job."

Lou Holtz achieved every one of those goals. This is probably where his belief and discipline for goal setting began. What his story taught me was the power of goal setting and that all goals are important but not equal. With storytelling it's the same. There are countless good stories you can tell about your business, your family, and your customers, but you need to know which stories are more important to share than others.

When creating their stories, I like to steer business owners toward what I have defined as the **Three Fs of storytelling: Fit, Feel, Faithful**. Step back one second and remember that your goal with storytelling is to get into the heart and change the mind. With that, we know some stories are more effective than others, but what makes them more effective at getting to the Heart? There is no magic to creating your story, but there are magical stories being told. The more you think about and develop your story, the better storyteller you will be. The Three Fs: Fit, Feel, Faithful will help you get started.

FIT: Stories about what your product or service "does for the customer."

How does your product or service fit into consumers' lives or lifestyles? How does your product or service make their lives better or easier? Approach it from the consumers' perspective. Do consumers want …

A mattress -or- a good night's sleep?
A mortgage -or- a place to call home?
A security system -or- protection?

See the distinction? When you look at it from the consumers' point of view, it becomes clear why shouting about your mattress sale every week doesn't get anyone's attention.

FEEL: Stories about how your product or service makes customers "feel."

Storytelling gets even more effective when you can *make people "feel."* Creatively, **FEEL** stories are a step beyond **FIT** stories because they dive right into the emotion in the situation. The difference between telling me about your mattress and talking to me about a good night's sleep is the difference between facts and emotion. Facts tell us, but emotions connect us. Connecting with consumers through emotions (versus facts) will get into hearts and forge bonds that create life-long customers. Think about **FEEL** in the following way.

FIT		**FEEL**
Good night's sleep	-to-	more energy to hang out with the family
Place to call home	-to-	a wonderful place to raise your family
Protection	-to-	peace of mind for protecting your loved ones

Great storytelling heads straight for the heart by connecting emotionally. You can connect through humor, sorrow, joy, etc. I personally like connecting my clients through humor. After years of storytelling, I know that humor enters the heart in a natural, easy, acceptable way. People will "allow you in" because they are connecting with what they are feeling. Good storytelling is the emotional bond between your business or service and consumers. It's more than just branding, it's bonding; remember this ... anytime you tickle the toes and touch the heart, you can change the mind.

FAITHFUL: Your faithful customers are your most powerful storytellers.

The absolute best person to tell your story is NOT YOU! You want your customers to be your storytellers! In today's hyper-connected world, Word of Mouth can spread like wildfire through customer reviews and testimonials. There are lots of articles, surveys, and studies regarding online reviews. In a nutshell, those resources tell us that 1) most people have become jaded and less trusting of traditional advertising; 2) overwhelmingly, people read online reviews before they check out a business or website; and

3) the trust factor is there as well with people saying they trust online reviews almost as much as personal recommendations. As a part of your strategy, bring your great online reviews and ratings to life by adding audio to them. The raw power and real emotion of the human voice is best. Start using that audio/customer testimonial on your website, YouTube, Radio, TV, etc.

Lesson #6

There are many stories you can share with consumers, but some are more effective at breaking through and connecting than others. You have to meet people where they are if you want to establish a relationship with them. Focus your marketing from the consumers' perspective. Use my **Three Fs: Fit, Feel, Faithful** framework to help you tickle the toes, touch the heart and change minds!

Brand building with Bricks & Mortar

THREE LITTLE PIGS HAPPILY BUILD THREE HOUSES, EACH BUILT WITH DIFFERENT MATERIALS: STRAW, STICKS, AND BRICKS. The big bad wolf rolls up on the houses and decides to destroy what each pig worked hard to build. He approaches the first house made of straw. He "huffs, and he puffs, and he blows the house down!" He goes to the second house. He takes a huge breath, sucking in as much hot air as he can, and then he blows hard at the house made of sticks and leaves the house in a pile on the ground! The big bad wolf, feeling overly confident, does a little happy dance and gets ready to blow away the third house. Once again, he huffs, and he puffs, and he huffs and puffs more, but no matter how much he tries, he can't blow away the house made of bricks.

The Three Little Pigs taught us what? Build with bricks! Imagine your brand is a house. What are you building your brand with? Are you building with materials that are solid, bonding, and permanent?

Be careful relying only on search engines to build your brand. This is like using straw, not memorable and "blows away easily!"

If you are attempting to build your brand with *Sales and limited-time offers*, you might as well be building with sticks, because your "sticks" (sales, facts, and numbers) are not memorable. There is nothing to connect or bond with. Plus, it's a short-term, low-margin strategy.

The last house standing was built with bricks. Storytelling builds your brand brick solid. Storytelling is memorable; it bonds and builds "permanent SEO (Search Engine Optimization)" in the minds of consumers. Storytelling is also a great strategy for moving you up from being grouped in part of an unbranded search for "insurance" to being a coveted, branded search for "GEICO.com"

Good storytelling, the kind that makes good businesses famous and bottom lines explode, doesn't happen by accident, and it doesn't happen overnight. Like any solid structure, a brand is built over time. You need strategy, preparation, and planning. Some years ago, I created a simple method called *Bricks & Mortar* to help business owners build and map out a storytelling plan.

We know both brick and mortar, working together, strengthen and give long life to a structure. Now, apply that same principle to building your story with Bricks & Mortar. The goal is to reinforce your brand in the minds of consumers, so much so that your business or service is top of mind. Built brick by brick, solid and made to last.

MORTAR

These elements are what you want to be known for. They don't change. These elements remain consistent throughout your marketing. Think of Mortar as the glue (the words or phrases) that binds your stories together.

> **WORDS/PHRASES:** These are the words or phrases you want to "own" in the minds of consumers. This is your DM. When I say your name in your market, what words will I hear back? When you have consumers repeating your DM, you know you are a top-of-mind leader in the marketplace.
>
> These great businesses "own" words/phrases and a place in the hearts and minds of consumers in their markets.
>
> - Firefighters Credit Union mortar: *The Money Man*
> - Kitchenland USA mortar: *Kitchens built in the tradition of my slightly obsessive Amish heritage*
> - Steve's Pest Control mortar: *You've got a friend in the pest control business*

LOGO: Visual logo. Your brand's consistent look and feel. Audio logo. Jingle, music, child laughter, animal sound, etc.

VOICE: A spokesperson or a consistent voice throughout your ads.

BRICKS

Each *Brick* represents an aspect of your business or service that will dramatize your DM. Brick elements change and evolve. You will be able to identify lots of *Bricks*, but remember my rule: **one brick, one story idea**. Got more to say ... do it with the next Brick. So, "*brick by brick*," you begin bonding with people through thought-provoking, humorous, engaging, written, voiced, emotional stories.

Here is an example of great Bricks & Mortar strategy from Steve's Pest Control. This shows you their Mortar, Bricks, and how they brought "one Brick" to life in a :60 second ad.

Steve's Pest Control
Bricks & Mortar Strategy

MORTAR
You've got a friend in the pest control business

BRICKS

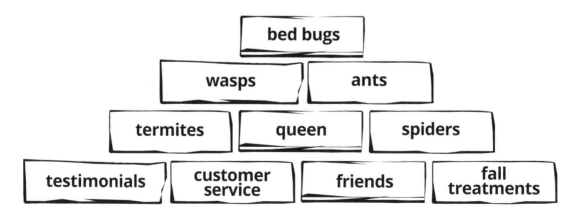

Steve's Pest Control Ad

Brick / Title: "Bed Bugs"

Writer: Johnny Molson

ANC: ITTY BITTY LITTLE DISGUSTING ICKY FEET. SIX OF THEM. SKITTERING BY YOUR HEAD WHILE YOU SLEEP. NESTLING DOWN AGAINST YOUR SKIN... AND DIVING IN FOR A BITE. THAT'S HOW BED BUGS LIVE, YA KNOW. OFF OF YOU. BED BUGS ARE LIKE THE VAMPIRES OF THE ARTHROPODS. DRINKING YOUR BLOOD WHILE YOU SLEEP. VAMPIRES. JUST NOT QUITE AS SEXY AS THOSE OLD TIMES MOVIES. SO ... IT SEEMS YOU HAVE TWO CHOICES. BURN EVERY BED AND PILLOW YOU OWN IN A GIGUNDUS FIRE ... OR CALL YOUR FRIEND STEVE.

STV: I'M STEVE FROM STEVE'S PEST CONTROL. IF YOU WANT BUGS REMOVED, ERADICATED, OR JUST OLD FASHIONED DEAD ... WE'RE GONNA SOLVE YOUR PEST PROBLEM. I GUARANTEE IT.

ANC: FROM THE TINIEST MITES TO THE MEANEST MOLES ... CALL STEVE'S PEST CONTROL. ONLINE AT STEVE'S PEST CONTROL "DOT" COM.

(jingle out – sing with music – mortar words) (*"... NOW YOU'VE GOT A FRIEND IN THE PEST CONTROL BUSINESS, STEVE'S PEST CONTROL."*)

Lesson #7

Some stories are more important to share than others for your business. Once you've got your DM, use my **Bricks & Mortar** method to prioritize your stories and keep your ongoing conversation on track.

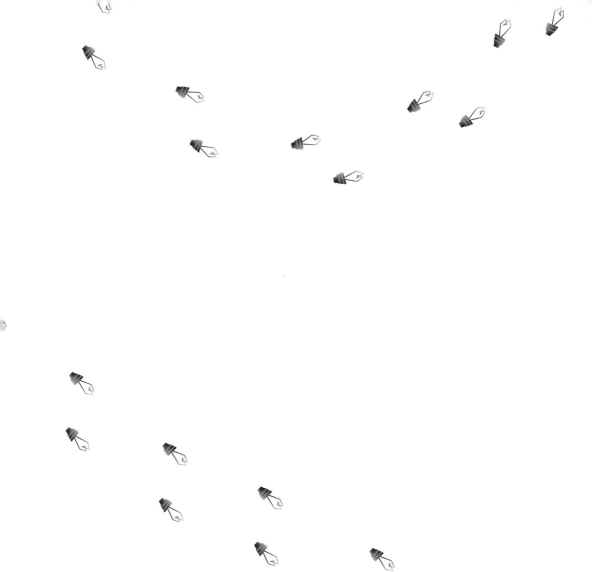

47

Parades or Stadiums

IMAGINE HANDING OUT 2,000 FLYERS TO A PARADE OF
DIFFERENT PEOPLE, EVERY DAY. Over the course of 30 days,
you've handed out 60,000 flyers. You've reached 60,000
different people ... congrats, your "reach" is good! But don't
pop the bubbly yet, because the response will be terrible. Why?
Because no one pays attention to a flyer handed to them, once,
as they're making their way to the office or home or to the big
game. You never really "reached" them!

Now picture a stadium filled with 2,000 yelling fans. You are able
to reach those same fans once every day for 30 days. You would

have still handed out 60,000 flyers, but the results would be so much better. Why? Because we know the repetition of saying the same thing, to the same group, over and over, breaks through the clutter. Pretty soon you may actually make a connection, and then a customer and, fingers crossed, a fan for life!

Marketing effectiveness is not about the size of the group you reach. It is about how many times you can "reach" the same group. Reach is useless without the PROVEN principles of frequency and repetition. A lot of good storytelling has failed simply because there wasn't "enough gas" (frequency) built into the plan.

Imagine building a nice, new pool in your backyard. You wouldn't start drilling a bunch of small holes around your backyard, would you? No, you would drill deep in one area. You want to drill deep with one group of people. Don't waste your hard earned media dollars going "wide and thin." Instead, focus on a group and go deep.

Lesson #8

We need to hear or see something repeatedly, over years, for that message to break through the clutter in our crazy, busy, daily lives. If we don't hear a message multiple times, that message never has a chance to get through. Think about how you connect with someone personally: you connect or bond with them when you talk more, share more, and spend more time together. That's how good storytelling works. You share your story with consumers, and over time a bond develops.

8 Lessons Recap

Lesson 1: Your brand is your promise to your customers. Don't make promises you can't keep.

Lesson 2: Start an ongoing conversation with your long-term relational buyers. That's where the money is.

Lesson 3: Leaders lead by example. Be a Leader in your category, and start sharing that story. People like to follow a leader.

Lesson 4: People remember stories, but they don't remember facts and numbers. Stories get into the heart in a way that facts and numbers never will.

8 Lessons Recap

Lesson 5: Clearly define your *Difference Maker*. It's your battle cry and should be included in all of your marketing.

Lesson 6: Tell consumers how you can improve their lives with the *Three Fs: Fit, Feel, Faithful*.

Lesson 7: Use Bricks & Mortar to help you stay on track with your storytelling. Your Mortar words will never change. Your Bricks will continually change. Remember my rule: one brick/ one story idea.

Lesson 8: Drill deep not wide. It's better to talk with a smaller group of people over and over, rather than a huge crowd once.

The Takeaway

A STUBBORN, OLD MAN WAS FACING THE WORST FLOOD IN A CENTURY. He had seen a lot of floods come and go in his 43 years at his old house, and he was determined to ride this one out like all the others.

The water was rising fast and beginning to seep into his house. A boat pulled up, and a neighbor yelled, "Come aboard now. The levee is going to break, and no one will be able to get in!" The old man replied, "No thanks, the Lord will save me." So, they moved on.

The water kept rising, and the old man had to move to the second floor. Looking out an upstairs window, he saw a canoe with townspeople coming by. "Jump in! The water is rising fast!," they screamed. The old man replied, "No thanks, the Lord is coming to save me!" So, they moved on.

The water kept rising until the old man was forced to move onto his roof! In minutes, his two-story house was completely under water. The poor old guy had to jump to a nearby tree limb and hang on for dear life. All of a sudden, a helicopter dropped out of the dark, stormy skies, and a crew member lowered a ladder down to the old man and shouted, "Old man, hold onto the ladder, and we'll pull you to safety!" The old man replied, "No thanks, I'm waiting here on the Lord." They flew away to help other survivors. The flood waters kept rising, and the man was washed away.

So now, the old guy is standing in front of St. Peter at the pearly gates, complaining, soaking wet, and mad. "I waited and waited for the Lord to save me. Telling one and all how great He is, how He was coming to save me. What happened, and why didn't He show up?"

St. Peter replied, "He sent you a boat, a canoe, and a helicopter. You dummy, what more did you want?"

Sometimes, the answers are right in front of us, and we fail to see them. Storytelling has been around for thousands of years for a good reason – it works. You're searching for a way to break through the clutter and grow your business.

Well, storytelling may be your boat, your canoe, or your helicopter – don't turn away, or you may miss the answer you've been looking for.

Tickle the toes,
Touch the hearts, and you, too,
Will change minds.

Acknowledgments

To the thousands of business owners and entrepreneurs that I have had the good fortune to partner with and strategize with over the years, thank you. Keep telling your stories and leading your categories!

To my very first marketing firm clients, Brad and Amanda Schrock, thank you for taking a leap of faith more than 15 years ago. You are great people and amazing business owners. Live long and prosper my good friends!

A special thanks to those who had a hand in making this book a reality: Jeff Delvaux, Collin Schlict, Jonathan Rand, Don Jacobs, Kelley McDonald, Gabby Ebron, Lou Holtz, Steve's Pest Control, Johnny Molson, Lynn DeGrande, and Roann Mefford.

I am eternally grateful to each and every one of you.

About the author

Chuck Mefford

Husband. Father. Great Lakes Sailor. Lifetime Packer fan. Rocket's #1 ball thrower. One of the dudes at Valley Creek Church running the music and message slides. Storyteller. Brand Strategist. Author. National Speaker.

About the illustrator

Collin Daniel Schlicht

Collin believes that he is a life-giving person, created to create life-giving art. He does so as a professional illustrator and graphic designer, but also just for fun. Collin lives with his beautiful wife Miriam in the great Pacific Northwest.

Chuck's Other Books

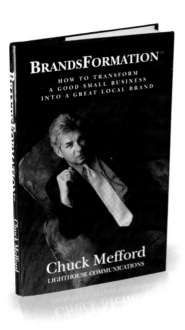

Order at amazon.com or brandsformation.com